Customer

Service

By L.M. Keatts

Copyright © 2015 by L.M. Keatts

Introduction

Several years ago I was working as a Sales Advisor for a major company in Pharr Texas. It was lunch time for most and within ear shot I overheard a very brief conversation that inspired me to sit down at my computer and write a much needed book for employee training.

Did you know that you hold the key to your future? In fact, you even hold the key to your next paycheck!

I have written this book on Customer Service because there is a missing element that needs to be addressed.

Customer Service begins with you!

Author

First Impression

The customer's first impression of you is up to you. Did you know that? It is the final key that will unlock your success. Whether you climb the ladder to the top or drop off in failure, everything falls in your lap.

From the time the customer makes their approach to the moment that customer walks away, they are reading you like a book. At that moment you do not have the time to prepare. Satisfied customers always return to the same store and to the same sales person, usually. There is an old adage that says, "I don't care what people think of me." **You need to care!**

In the retail industry your attitude plays a very vital role. How people perceive you is how they will receive you. Good or bad. Let me say that again.

How others perceive you is how they will receive you.

Time Clock Mentality

Your attitude from the moment you step from your car to the time you walk out the front door should be with the customer in mind. I want to give you two examples that I believe will help you to see this very valuable point.

❖ Jim has been working since 6am with no break in between. His watch reads 2:30 and he is really looking forward to a few minutes of relaxation.

He clocks out and heads for the back door. But before Jim reaches the back door an elderly lady makes her approach. Jim is tired. It is the company policy to give him a 30 minute break. To address the need of the customer will take away some much needed time. Jim thinks it through and decides to ignore her request and demises her.

The customer leaves the store offended and takes her business elsewhere.

❖ Jim has been on the clock since 6am this morning without as much as a break. He is grateful just to get a 30 minute lunch break. Heading for the back door Jim is approached. Instead of ignoring the customer he takes the time needed to assist her and in the process he lost about 10 minutes. Two weeks later that same customer is back shopping again.

You have two options that you can take if this ever happens to you.

- Assist the customer
- Locate someone

Satisfied customers always return to the same store and much of the time to that same sales person!

It's all in the attitude. 70% of those that work in retail have fallen far short. That can change and it can change with you.

Customer service is not at the front counter. Customer service is helping a customer with their needs before they get to the front counter!

Take the time to notice if you can be of assistance to someone and always make yourself available.

Get Involved

Get so involved in your company that you begin to have a vision for them. When you get a vision for your company that's when you will come to work with the customer in mind. Perhaps you have a job where you have to meet a certain quota each day. You can't have those sales numbers if you have dissatisfied customers. You can't meet your quota if you ignore the needs of your customers.

Satisfaction is not based on what someone can do for you but rather on what you can do for others. If you will change your attitude you will change your paycheck!

I understand that sometimes in the work place customers are not always pleasant to be around. Sometimes they wake up in the mornings with an attitude. But that shouldn't matter.

Our job is to provide a service to the public. That is the vision of any company. I have found that you can usually change a customer's demeanor by simply showing an interest in them.

"Take the time to address unhappy customers and do everything in your power to remedy the situation. It's not only worth keeping their business, but also avoiding any negative word of mouth exposure."

White House Office of Consumer Affairs

Just recently I read that 67% of customers hung up the phone out of frustration because they couldn't speak to a real person.

It should never get to that level. As employees in retail we are responsible for the needs of our customers. And if you think otherwise then you need to find another job!

That's why it is so **imperative** to be available and to **invest** that extra time, even if we lose 15 minutes of our lunch break.

Liability or Asset

Are you a liability to your company? Or are you an asset?

An individual that is a liability to his company is only there for a paycheck. Let me say it again, **your pay scale changes when your attitude changes.**

Door Greeter

In most big chain stores the door greeter is a person that just hands out coupon books. Your job is to **greet** and **meet** them not just hand them a coupon book! When they walk through the front door make yourself available. Never yell across the store, "Welcome to..."

- Let them know that you are there to help them if they need anything.

- Tell them how much you value their business.

❖ If I walk through the front door and you fail to properly greet me, I will report you.

❖ If I approach you for help and you ignore and dismiss me because you have only 10 minutes left on your break, I will report you.

❖ If you're talking on your cell phone and I have to go out of my way to get your attention, I will report you.

What any retail company simply cannot afford is to lose an existing customer. That is a customer that has shopped in their store for years.

❖ Never think that you can't be replaced.

- ❖ Never assume that what you say will be counted higher than the customer.

- ❖ The customer is always right.

Red Carpet Treatment

I have seen how important people are treated at retail stores.

Customer service is number one priority when the Mayor walks in. That should be the case when everyone walks in!

Before we draw to a close I think we should go back over some of the material that we have covered.

- ❖ **The customer's first impression of you is up to you. How others perceive you is how they will receive you.**

- ❖ **Satisfied customers always return to the same store and usually to the same sales person.**

- ❖ **Customer Service is not at the front counter it is standing right in front of you.**

- ❖ **When you get a vision for your company you will get a vision for your customer.**

❖ Satisfaction is not based on what others can do for you but rather what you can do for others.

❖ It is imperative to be available and to invest that extra time even if you lose 15 minutes of your lunch break.

❖ Are you a liability to your company or are you an asset?

❖ Usually we stick a coupon book in someone's hand and wish them well. We should meet them and greet them!

❖ What any retail company simply cannot afford is to lose an existing customer.

❖ Red Carpet treatment should be for every one walking through the front door.

❖ Change your attitude and your pay check will change.

- The Probability of selling to an existing customer is 60-70%. The probability to selling to a new prospect is 5-20%.
  -Marketing Metrics

- For every customer complaint there are 26 unhappy customers who have remained silent.
  -Lee Resource

- 96% of unhappy customers don't complain, however 91% of those will simply leave and never come back.
  -₁Financial Training Services

- 70% of employees are "disengaged", meaning they're no longer committed to the company. It's evident in positions from executives officers to front-line employees this "I don't care" attitude is hurting businesses in a big way.
  -The Gallup Organization Researches

The highest form of customer service in any business is to treat each one as a dear friend. If you simply cannot do that then you will never excel in business!

I have worked for several big store chains and not one of them offered any training in customer service. They just basically threw you out on the sales floor and you had to paddle the boat the best way you could!

Never get caught unprepared. At all cost you have to be very certain of your position. Customers become offended very easily and once you offend a customer it becomes very complicated after that.

Customers are the greatest asset for any business. We should really go out of our way to make their time in our store very enjoyable and pleasant. This book was written with you in mind. You are the key to a sufficiently operated business.

For the next 31 days I want you to apply everything in this book and document your sales on a daily basis. If you are required to have a certain quota each day this should be documented as well. If you will follow the path in this book I believe that you will see an enormous difference in your sales and perhaps in your paycheck as well.

Documented Sales:

Total:

Quota:

Total:

Notes:

Documented sales:

Total:

Quota:

Total:

Notes:

Documented Sales:

Total:

Quota:

Total:

Notes:

Documented Sales:

Total:

Quota:

Total:

Notes:

Documented Sales:

Total:

Quota:

Total:

Notes:

Documented Sales:

Total:

Quota:

Total:

Notes:

Documented Sales:

Total:

Quota:

Total:

Notes:

Documented Sales:

Total:

Quota:

Total:

Notes:

Documented Sales:

Total:

Quota:

Total:

Notes:

Documented Sales:

Total:

Quota:

Total:

Notes:

Documented Sales:

Total:

Quota:

Total:

Notes:

Documented Sales:

Total:

Quota:

Total:

Notes:

Documented Sales:

Total:

Quota:

Total:

Notes:

Sales Journal   Day 14

Documented Sales:

Total:

Quota:

Total:

Notes:

Documented Sales:

Total:

Quota:

Total:

Notes:

Documented Sales:

Total:

Quota:

Total:

Notes:

Documented Sales:

Total:

Quota:

Total:

Notes:

Documented Sales:

Total:

Quota:

Total:

Notes:

Documented Sales:

Total:

Quota:

Total:

Notes:

Documented Sales:

Total:

Quota:

Total:

Notes:

Documented Sales:

Total:

Quota:

Total:

Notes:

Documented Sales:

Total:

Quota:

Total:

Notes:

Documented Sales:

Total:

Quota:

Total:

Notes:

Documented Sales:

Total:

Quota:

Total:

Notes:

Documented Sales:

Total:

Quota:

Total:

Notes:

Documented Sales:

Total:

Quota:

Total:

Notes:

Documented Sales:

Total:

Quota:

Total:

Notes:

Documented Sales:

Total:

Quota:

Total:

Notes:

Documented Sales:

Total:

Quota:

Total:

Notes:

Documented Sales:

Total:

Quota:

Total:

Notes:

Documented Sales:

Total:

Quota:

Total:

Notes:

www.ingramcontent.com/pod-product-compliance
Lightning Source LLC
Chambersburg PA
CBHW071546170526
45166CB00004B/1571